MW00901522

Aunt,
~ tell me ~
your story

Dear aunt,

ⸯⸯⸯ

I offer you this diary so that you can give me the greatest gift: the gift of your life story and experience.

I know and love the person you are today through your role as an aunt, but I would also like to discover your other facets and the different phases that have marked your life and made you the woman you are today.

All you have to do is give me back this diary filled with your most personal thoughts, anecdotes and memories. You can either fill it out with me or do it on your own.

Feel free to skip any question you don't want to answer. They have been thought of to guide your life testimony, and can be completed with your own reflections at the end of the diary and embellished with your most beautiful pictures!

Once you have finished your story, I will keep this memory book carefully and treasure it.

I hope you will take as much pleasure in filling it out as I will in reading it.

 Thank you very much

♡

SPECIAL REQUEST

Dear Customers,
Thank you for your trust.
I'm an independent
publisher.

If you like this Journal, feel free to leave me a

comment on Amazon. I read each one of your

comments with pleasure: they are crucial to

support my work and allow me to provide you

with new quality content. I hope you will enjoy

this journal as much as I

enjoyed designing it !

In order not to miss any of my next publications,
I suggest you to scan this QR code and click on
"+ Follow" on my author page :

Thank you very much in advance !

Erika Rossi

SUMMARY

YOU

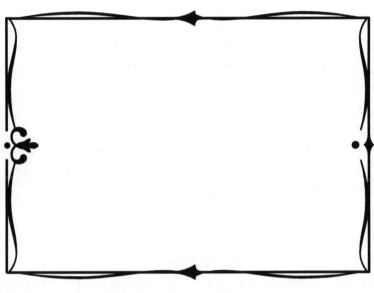

Your name is

....

How did your parents choose your name ?

....

....

Today; ...., you have .... children, ...
grandchildren and .... great-
grandchildren .

You were born on .... in ....

YOUR ROOTS

(Complete with the names and dates of birth
of your ancestors)

Our best picture ♡

YOUR YOUTH

Did you like going to school ? Did you do well or was it hard for you ?

_____
_____
_____
_____
_____
_____
_____

What were your favorite and least favorite subjects ? Are there any subjects that don't exist anymore ?

_____
_____
_____
_____
_____
_____
_____
_____
_____
_____

Who were your favorite teachers and why ?

Who were your best friends ? What are your best memories with them ?

What did you play in the playground ?

When you misbehaved, how were you punished ? How often were you punished ?

As a child, what was the job you wanted to do when you grew up ?

What were your favorite games/toys ? How did you spend your free time ?

How did your parents describe you ?

Did you have pets ? If not, do you wish you had ?

What was your nickname ? Why did they call you that ?

What did you do during school vacation ?
If you went away, who did you go with and where ?

What was the biggest mistake you made as a child ?

_____
_____
_____
_____
_____
_____

What was your favorite book ?

_____
_____

What was your favorite food ? What was your least favorite food ?

_____
_____

Tell me the funniest memory of your childhood.

_____
_____
_____
_____
_____
_____
_____
_____

Did you help a lot at home ? What did you do ?

Which birthday is your most special memory ?

Did you have any special family traditions ? What were the family celebrations like and which ones did you prefer ?

What are the happiest memories of your childhood ?

A picture of you as a child ♡

A picture of you as a child ♡

As a teenager, what did you do with your friends ? Did you go out a lot? Did you keep your childhood friends ?

Overall, did you enjoy your adolescence ? What are your best memories ?

Have you pursued your studies ? If so, what did you study ?

A picture of you as a teenager
♡

YOUR FAMILY

Tell me about your parents: what were their jobs ? Describe their
habits and their respective characters. What memories do you
have with them ?

Your mom :

_____

_____

_____

_____

_____

_____

_____

_____

_____

_____

_____

_____

_____

_____

_____

_____

_____

_____

_____

Your dad :

23

A picture of your parents
♡

What did your grandparents do and what were they like ?
How often did you see them ? What did you like to do with
them or at their house ? Did they teach you anything ?

A picture of your maternal grandparents

A picture of your paternal grandparents ♡

What do you know about your great-grandparents and more
distant ancestors ?
Does your family have a particular ethnic background ?

_____

_____

_____

_____

_____

_____

_____

_____

_____

_____

Where did you live with your family and what was your home like ?

_____

_____

_____

_____

_____

_____

_____

_____

_____

_____

Are you close with my mom/dad ?
Do you have any memorable stories about her/him ?
What is your relationship with your other brothers/sisters like
? Describe them to me.

A picture of your whole family ♡

YOUR ADULTHOOD

As a young adult, what were your best skills ? Which were you best at ?

_____

_____

_____

_____

_____

_____

What principles passed on by your parents have guided your adult life ?

_____

_____

_____

_____

_____

What jobs did you have ? Did you enjoy them ? If you could have started over, would you have chosen the same work ?

_____

_____

Have you ever been on a long journey ? Where did you travel ?
What are your favorite travel memories ?

Have you gone through particularly difficult times in your life ? How did you cope with them ? Did you experience historical moments when you were younger (war, crisis...)?

Tell me : when and how did you meet your current parnter ?

Tell me more about him (/her).

How many serious relationships have you had in your life?
What can you tell me about them ?

How did you know that your current relationship was special ?

If you are married : how did the proposal go ?

What was your wedding like ?
Did you go on honeymoon afterwards ?

If you are a mom : how did you decide to have a child ?

What is your best memory with your partner ?

A picture of both of you

At what age did you get your driver's licence ? And your first car ? Do you have a funny story about it ?

What is the best gift you have ever received ?

Have you participated in any contests or competitions in your life ?

_____
_____
_____
_____
_____
_____
_____
_____
_____
_____

How has your perception and experience of femininity evolved over the years ? What makes you feel like a "woman" today ?

_____
_____
_____
_____
_____
_____
_____
_____
_____
_____
_____

YOUR LIFE AS A MOM

[To be completed if you are a mother

How did you react when you found out you were pregnant ? What about your partner ?

....
....
....
....
....
....

What was your first pregnancy like ? What about childbirth ? If there were several, were you apprehensive about the next ones ?

....
....
....
....
....
....
....
....
....
....
....
....

How was your first year of motherhood ?

_____
_____
_____
_____
_____
_____
_____
_____
_____

How did you balance your family life and work obligations ? If you could have started over, would you have done it the same way ?

_____
_____
_____
_____
_____
_____
_____
_____
_____
_____

What did (/do) you enjoy doing most with your children ?

How did you choose your children's names ? Do they have a particular meaning? What were your other favorite names ?

What was the biggest mistake your children made ?

_____
_____
_____
_____
_____
_____
_____

Is there anything you experienced when you were younger that you promised yourself you wouldn't put your own children through ?

_____
_____
_____
_____
_____
_____
_____

What do you like the most about being a mom ?

_____
_____
_____
_____
_____
_____

42

What is the most tiring / difficult thing about being a mom ?

What are your most beautiful memories with your kids ?

Pictures of you ♡

YOUR LIFE AS AN AUNT

How did you feel when you found out you were going to be an aunt ?

_____
_____
_____
_____
_____
_____

What memories do you have of my birth and me as a baby ?

_____
_____
_____
_____
_____
_____
_____
_____

What is your favorite part of being an aunt ?

What are your favorite activities to do with me ?

Are there things about me that remind you of yourself ? Do
we have anything in common ?

Is there anything you've always wanted to tell me ?

What are your most beautiful memories with me ?

Pictures of us ♡

YOUR CURRENT LIFE

What are your current favorite activities ?

What are your daily rituals ?

Who are the people you feel closest to today ?

_____

_____

_____

_____

_____

_____

_____

_____

Is there anything I don't know about you that would surprise me ?

_____

_____

_____

_____

_____

_____

_____

_____

_____

What are your favorite books and writers ?

What are your favorite movies and actors ?

What are your favorite music styles and singers ?

If you won the lottery tomorrow, what would you do ?
(You can let your imagination run wild !)

_____
_____
_____
_____
_____
_____
_____
_____
_____
_____
_____
_____

What would you do if you only had one day left to live ?

_____
_____
_____
_____
_____
_____
_____
_____

Are there any skills / knowledge you would like to learn ?

_____
_____
_____
_____
_____
_____
_____
_____
_____
_____
_____

According to you, what are the inventions that have most revolutionized the course of humankind ?

_____
_____
_____
_____
_____
_____
_____
_____

You and your relatives now ♡

RETROSPECTIVE OF YOUR LIFE

Where did you like living the most and why ? Would you have liked to live somewhere else ?

_____

_____

_____

_____

_____

_____

_____

_____

_____

_____

_____

_____

_____

_____

_____

_____

_____

_____

_____

_____

_____

_____

_____

Throughout your life, who have been your different role models or, a source of inspiration for you (relatives or celebrities) ?

What are you most proud of ? What experiences have been the most important in your life and have made you the person you are today ?

Do you have any regrets ? Do you wish you had done things differently ? What do you wish you had spent less time on ? What about more time on ?

What dreams have you achieved ? Are there any particular things you would like to accomplish ?

How do you imagine your retirement ? If you are already retired, what do you prefer in this phase of your life ?

What are the happiest events and memories in your life ?

What would you like to be remembered for ? What values are most important to you ? What legacy would you like to leave ?

What advice would you give me regarding my personal and professional life ?

I'D ALSO LIKE TO KNOW...

Your favorites tips & recipes

Your favorites tips & recipes

Your favorites tips & recipes

Your favorites tips & recipes

Your favorites tips & recipes

Your favorites tips & recipes

Your favorites tips & recipes

A little love note ...

From me to you :

From you to me :

Your life in pictures ♡

Your life in pictures ♡

Your life in pictures ♡

Your life in pictures ♡

Your life in pictures ♡

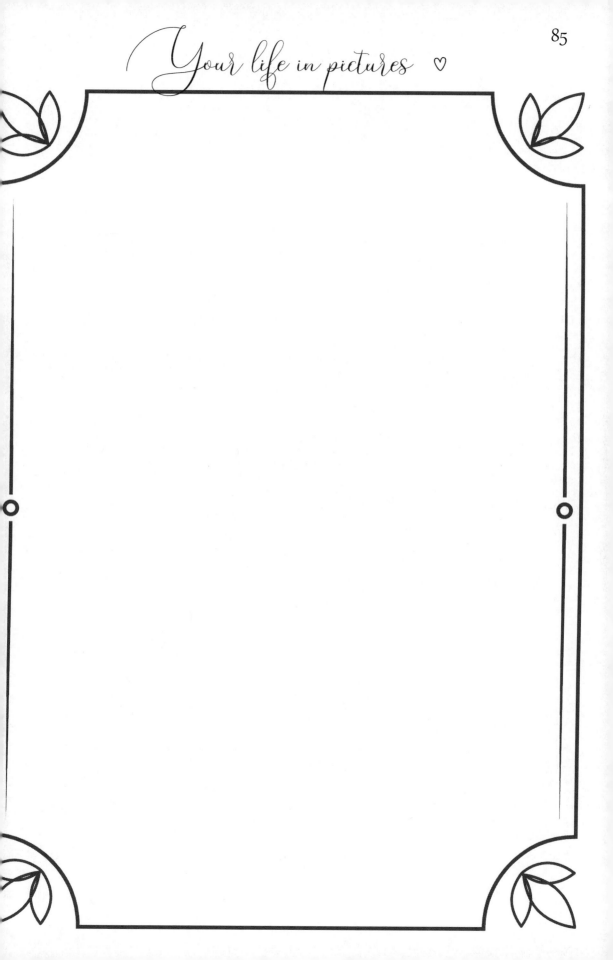

Your life in pictures ♡

Your life in pictures ♡

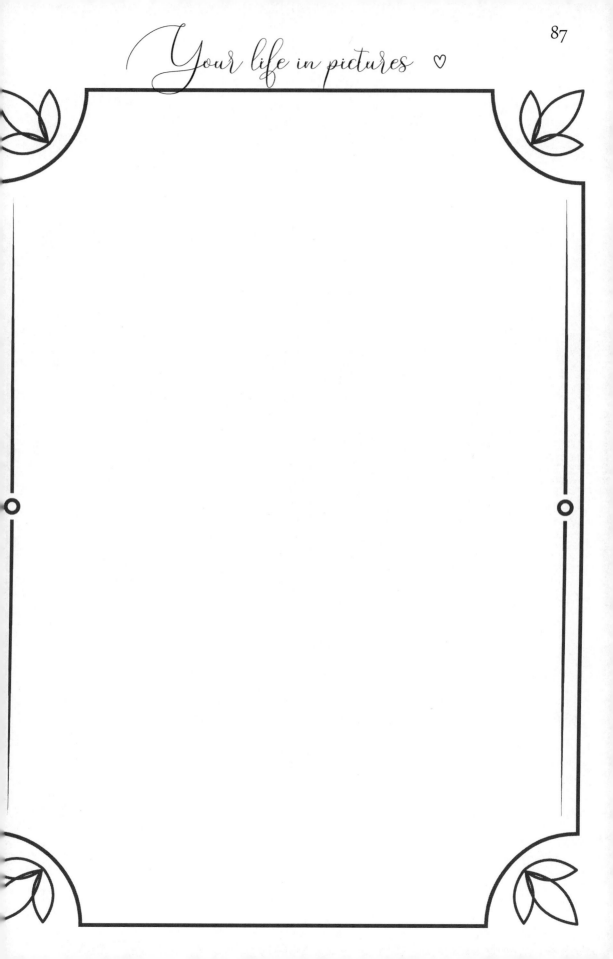

Your life in pictures ♡

Your life in pictures ♡

Your life in pictures ♡

Your life in pictures ♡

Your life in pictures ♡

Your life in pictures ♡

Your life in pictures ♡

Your life in pictures ♡

Your life in pictures ♡

EXTRA NOTES

Also available on amazon.com
-ERIKA ROSSI-

« Tell me your story » Collection

Grandpa tell me your story : Keepsake memory journal to be filled by your grandfather with the story of his life

Grandma tell me your story : Keepsake memory journal to be filled by your grandmother with the story of her life

Dad tell me your story : Keepsake memory journal to be filled by your father with the story of his life

Godmother tell me your story : Keepsake memory journal to be filled by your godmother with the story of her life

Godfather tell me your story : Keepsake memory journal to be filled by your godfather with the story of his life

Aunt tell me your story : Keepsake memory journal to be filled by your auntie with the story of her life

Uncle tell me your story : Keepsake memory journal to be filled by your uncle with the story of his life

« Gratitude journals » Collection

Lamaste - Gratitude journal for Kids : 3 minute Daily Journal Writing Prompts for Children to practice Gratitude & Mindfulness with Positive Affirmations, Quotes & Challenges